# 100
# POEMS TO
# HELP YOU
# HEAL

# 100 POEMS TO HELP YOU HEAL

EDITED BY LIZ ISON

BATSFORD

# Introduction

Many of us turn to poetry during difficult times in our lives because poems can offer us sustenance, consolation or perspective. Reading poetry can create a space in which to breathe, to feel, to sigh or to weep. In this collection are 100 potential poem-friends for you to get to know: perhaps you will find a poem that resonates, that articulates something of what you are feeling. Maybe you will experience a moment of comfort or a flash of enlightenment during the darker days. Poetry may help to move us towards peace or acceptance, or the beginnings of the thought that this *could* be a possibility, even if those feelings prove to be difficult or momentary.

However, this book of poems does not work like a prescription or some kind of biblio-cure making the pain of loss or grief vanish. There are no short cuts along the unique journeys we are compelled to undertake following a loss. Healing takes time and there can be bumps on the road. Though most of us will eventually find some accommodation with our loss, we can never really return to how things were before. We can, nevertheless, find refuge in the community of poetry, knowing ultimately that each poem reaches out, encouraging us to remember that we are not alone.

If you come across a poem that irritates or vexes, do not worry: you could try to work out why it's making you feel like that. You could also simply put it aside: self-care and kindness are what are important in these difficult days. Poems allow us to explore the contours and edges of private grief with more clarity or honesty. We could imagine the poem as a gift for ourselves: a gift of friendship, given in a spirit of kindness and of fellow-feeling. And perhaps from such spaces and from such gifts, healing may happen. Which ones will you come back to? Will you find a poem that you'd like to read aloud to a friend, or one you might pass on to someone who needs it?

Finding the words for nebulous, overwhelming feelings doesn't come easily. Gerard Manley Hopkins' writing, however, takes us to places few other writers can reach, creating searing descriptions of the pain and despair of deep grief ('Pitched past pitch of grief, / More pangs will, schooled at forepangs, wilder wring'), while also recognizing the potential for recovery in that tantalizing phrase: 'leave comfort root-room'. George Herbert, 17th–century priest and poet, tries shutting out his grief altogether, locking his heart away ('within my heart I made / Closets'); but however hard he tries, grief finds a way of seeping into his being.

Maya Angelou evokes the image of a great tree falling to describe the process of massive change that is set off after a loss ('Our souls, / dependent upon their/nurture, now shrink, wizened') but healing does follow ('after a period peace blooms, / slowly and always / irregularly'). That sense of occasional or irregular normality that can return unbidden – sensations which can sometimes cause guilt – is also captured well by William Wordsworth in the sonnet that starts 'Surprised by joy', which is followed by the realisation that his young daughter is no longer there to share the special moment.

Shakespeare can always be trusted to put into words the complexities and depths of human experience. In the extract from *Henry VI, Part 3*, Shakespeare explores the contrasting and overwhelming reactions of two brothers whose father has been murdered: one weeping, the other angry and vengeful ('I cannot weep, for all my body's moisture / Scarce serves to quench my furnace-burning heart'). In *Much Ado about Nothing*, Shakespeare turns his gaze to the role of those who console the bereaved. Leonato rails against the well-meaning friends who give out advice and try to comfort him. He rejects those who try to 'patch grief with proverbs'. If you are not going through the experience yourself ('tasting it'), you surely cannot understand.

In contrast, William Blake ('On Another's Sorrow') articulates the impulse of wanting to help those in distress: 'Can I see another's grief, / And not seek for kind relief?' To feel surrounded by family, friends or community certainly can make a difference. Emily Dickinson's heartfelt short poem 'Mama never forgets her birds', apparently penned for her cousins to help them come to terms with the death of their mother, like so many other poems in the collection, is not just a poem but, when read, when shared, becomes the very act of consolation.

Confronting our loss may help us draw on inner resources we didn't know we possessed. Rilke's line 'What batters you becomes your strength', or Claude McKay's assertion: 'I shall return again; I shall return to laugh and love' articulate this developing resilience.

There is no doubt that the experience of grief and the process of healing are complex, and vary for each person. For one of the most profound and sustained poetic explorations of grief ever written we turn to Lord Alfred Tennyson's *In Memoriam A.H.H.* This is a nearly three-thousand-line personal meditation on loss written following the death of Tennyson's best friend Arthur Hallam who died at the age of 22. It took Tennyson seventeen years to compose and edit the 133 cantos. There is only space to include excerpts of this most profound and sustained exploration of grief, but I believe it is worth spending time with its four most famous lines:

> I hold it true, whate'er befall;
> I feel it, when I sorrow most;
> 'Tis better to have loved and lost
> Than never to have loved at all.

# Let This Darkness Be a Bell Tower
*Sonnets to Orpheus*, Book II, 29

Quiet friend who has come so far,
feel how your breathing makes more space
  around you.
Let this darkness be a bell tower
and you the bell. As you ring,

what batters you becomes your strength.
Move back and forth into the change.
What is it like, such intensity of pain?
If the drink is bitter, turn yourself to wine.

In this uncontainable night,
be the mystery at the crossroads of your senses,
the meaning discovered there.

And if the world has ceased to hear you,
say to the silent earth: I flow.
To the rushing water, speak: I am.

Rainer Maria Rilke (1875–1926)
Translated from the German by Joanna Macy and
Anita Barrows

# 'Tis better to have loved and lost than never to have loved at all
Canto XXVII, *In Memoriam A. H. H.*

I envy not in any moods
    The captive void of noble rage,
    The linnet born within the cage,
That never knew the summer woods:

I envy not the beast that takes
    His license in the field of time,
    Unfetter'd by the sense of crime,
To whom a conscience never wakes;

Nor, what may count itself as blest,
    The heart that never plighted troth
    But stagnates in the weeds of sloth;
Nor any want-begotten rest.

I hold it true, whate'er befall;
    I feel it, when I sorrow most;
    'Tis better to have loved and lost
Than never to have loved at all.

Alfred, Lord Tennyson (1809–1892)

# In Blackwater Woods

Look, the trees
are turning
their own bodies
into pillars

of light,
are giving off the rich
fragrance of cinnamon
and fulfillment,

the long tapers
of cattails
are bursting and floating away over
the blue shoulders

of the ponds,
and every pond,
no matter what its
name is, is

nameless now.
Every year
everything
I have ever learned

in my lifetime
leads back to this: the fires
and the black river of loss
whose other side

is salvation,
whose meaning
none of us will ever know.
To live in this world

you must be able
to do three things:
to love what is mortal;
to hold it

against your bones knowing
your own life depends on it;
and, when the time comes to let it go,
to let it go.

Mary Oliver (1935–2019)

# Silence

Since I lost you I am silence-haunted;
    Sounds wave their little wings
A moment, then in weariness settle
    On the flood that soundless swings.

Whether the people in the street
    Like pattering ripples go by,
Or whether the theatre sighs and sighs
    With a loud, hoarse sigh:

Or the wind shakes a ravel of light
    Over the dead-black river,
Or night's last echoing
    Makes the daybreak shiver:

I feel the silence waiting
    To take them all up again
In its last completeness, swathing
    The noise of men.

D. H. Lawrence (1885–1930)

# After great pain, a formal feeling comes

After great pain, a formal feeling comes –
The Nerves sit ceremonious, like Tombs –
The stiff Heart questions 'was it He, that bore,'
And 'Yesterday, or Centuries before'?

The Feet, mechanical, go round –
A Wooden way
Of Ground, or Air, or Ought –
Regardless grown,
A Quartz contentment, like a stone –

This is the Hour of Lead –
Remembered, if outlived,
As Freezing persons, recollect the Snow –
First – Chill – then Stupor – then the letting go –

Emily Dickinson (1830-1886)

# He Prefers Her Earthly

This after-sunset is a sight for seeing,
Cliff-heads of craggy cloud surrounding it.
    – And dwell you in that glory-show?
You may; for there are strange strange things in
  being,
        Stranger than I know.

Yet if that chasm of splendour claim your presence
Which glows between the ash cloud and the dun,
    How changed must be your mortal mould!
Changed to a firmament-riding earthless essence
        From what you were of old:

All too unlike the fond and fragile creature
Then known to me … Well, shall I say it plain?
    I would not have you thus and there,
But still would grieve on, missing you, still feature
        You as the one you were.

Thomas Hardy (1840–1928)

'the earth had darkened and grown still'

**Twilight (Nahant)**
Sara Teasdale

# Wait

Wait, for now.
Distrust everything if you have to.
But trust the hours. Haven't they
carried you everywhere, up to now?
Personal events will become interesting again.
Hair will become interesting.
Pain will become interesting.
Buds that open out of season will become interesting.
Second-hand gloves will become lovely again;
their memories are what give them
the need for other hands. The desolation
of lovers is the same: that enormous emptiness
carved out of such tiny beings as we are
asks to be filled; the need
for the new love *is* faithfulness to the old.

Wait.
Don't go too early.
You're tired. But everyone's tired.
But no one is tired enough.
Only wait a little and listen:
music of hair,
music of pain,
music of looms weaving our loves again.
Be there to hear it, it will be the only time,
most of all to hear your whole existence,
rehearsed by the sorrows, play itself into total
    exhaustion.

Galway Kinnell (1927–2014)

'what thou art may never be destroyed'

No Coward Soul is Mine
Emily Brontë

# Confession

Lines 1-6

O what a cunning guest
Is this same grief! within my heart I made
Closets; and in them many a chest;
And like a master in my trade,
In those chests, boxes; in each box, a till:
Yet grief knows all, and enters when he will.

George Herbert (1593-1633)

# Give sorrow words
From *Macbeth*, Act IV, Scene iii

Give sorrow words. The grief that does not speak
Whispers the o'erfraught heart and bids it break.

William Shakespeare (1564-1616)

# Renouncement

I must not think of thee; and, tired yet strong,
I shun the thought that lurks in all delight –
The thought of thee – and in the blue heaven's
  height,
And in the sweetest passage of a song.
Oh, just beyond the fairest thoughts that throng
This breast, the thought of thee waits hidden yet
  bright;
But it must never, never come in sight;
I must stop short of thee the whole day long.

But when sleep comes to close each difficult day,
When night gives pause to the long watch I keep,
And all my bonds I needs must loose apart,
Must doff my will as raiment laid away, –
With the first dream that comes with the first sleep
    I run, I run, I am gathered to thy heart.

Alice Meynell (1847-1922)

# Solace

My window opens out into the trees
And in that small space
Of branches and of sky
I see the seasons pass
Behold the tender green
Give way to darker heavier leaves.
The glory of the autumn comes
When steeped in mellow sunlight
The fragile, golden leaves
Against a clear blue sky
Linger in the magic of the afternoon
And then reluctantly break off
And filter down to pave
A street with gold.
Then bare, gray branches
Lift themselves against the
Cold December sky
Sometimes weaving a web
Across the rose and dusk of late sunset
Sometimes against a frail new moon
And one bright star riding
A sky of that dark, living blue
Which comes before the heaviness
Of night descends, or the stars

Have powdered the heavens.
Winds beat against these trees;
The cold, but gentle rain of spring
Touches them lightly
The summer torrents strive
To lash them into a fury
And seek to break them –
But they stand.
My life is fevered
And a restlessness at times
An agony – again a vague
And baffling discontent
Possesses me.
I am thankful for my bit of sky
And trees, and for the shifting
Pageant of the seasons.
Such beauty lays upon the heart
A quiet.
Such eternal change and permanence
Take meaning from all turmoil
And leave serenity
Which knows no pain.

Clarissa Scott Delany (1901–1927)

# Sweet Evenings Come and Go, Love

Sweet evenings come and go, love,
  They came and went of yore:
This evening of our life, love,
  Shall go and come no more.

When we have passed away, love,
  All things will keep their name;
But yet no life on earth, love,
  With ours will be the same.

The daisies will be there, love,
  The stars in heaven will shine:
I shall not feel thy wish, love,
  Nor thou my hand in thine.

A better time will come, love,
  And better souls be born:
I would not be the best, love,
  To leave thee now forlorn.


George Eliot (1819-1880)

# Spleen

I was not sorrowful, I could not weep,
And all my memories were put to sleep.

I watched the river grow more white and strange,
All day till evening I watched it change.

All day till evening I watched the rain
Beat wearily upon the window pane

I was not sorrowful, but only tired
Of everything that ever I desired.

Her lips, her eyes, all day became to me
The shadow of a shadow utterly.

All day mine hunger for her heart became
Oblivion, until the evening came,

And left me sorrowful, inclined to weep,
With all my memories that could not sleep.

Ernest Dowson (1867-1900)

# Ailey, Baldwin, Floyd, Killens, and Mayfield

When great trees fall,
rocks on distant hills shudder,
lions hunker down
in tall grasses,
and even elephants
lumber after safety.

When great trees fall
in forests,
small things recoil into silence,
their senses
eroded beyond fear.

When great souls die,
the air around us becomes
light, rare, sterile.
We breathe, briefly.
Our eyes, briefly,
see with
a hurtful clarity.
Our memory, suddenly sharpened,
examines,
gnaws on kind words
unsaid,
promised walks
never taken.

Great souls die and
our reality, bound to

them, takes leave of us.
Our souls,
dependent upon their
nurture,
now shrink, wizened.
Our minds, formed
and informed by their
radiance,
fall away.
We are not so much maddened
as reduced to the unutterable ignorance of
dark, cold
caves.

And when great souls die,
after a period peace blooms,
slowly and always
irregularly. Spaces fill
with a kind of
soothing electric vibration.
Our senses, restored, never
to be the same, whisper to us.
They existed. They existed.
We can be. Be and be
better. For they existed.

Maya Angelou (1928–2014)

# Dreamland

When midnight mists are creeping,
    And all the land is sleeping,
Around me tread the mighty dead,
    And slowly pass away.

Lo, warriors, saints, and sages,
    From out the vanished ages,
With solemn pace and reverend face
    Appear and pass away.

The blaze of noonday splendour,
    The twilight soft and tender,
May charm the eye: yet they shall die,
    Shall die and pass away.

But here, in Dreamland's centre,
    No spoiler's hand may enter,
These visions fair, this radiance rare,
    Shall never pass away.

I see the shadows falling,
    The forms of old recalling;
Around me tread the mighty dead,
    And slowly pass away.

Lewis Carroll (1832-1898)

## First Great Sorrow

From *Adam Bede*

There is no despair
So absolute
As that which comes
With the first moments
Of our first great sorrow –

When we have not yet known
What it is to have suffered
    And be healed,
To have despaired
    And to have recovered hope.

George Eliot (1819–1880)

# Open Windows

Out of the window a sea of green trees
 Lift their soft boughs like the arms of a dancer,
They beckon and call me, 'Come out in the sun!'
 But I cannot answer.

I am alone with Weakness and Pain,
 Sick abed and June is going,
I cannot keep her, she hurries by
 With the silver-green of her garments blowing.

Men and women pass in the street
 Glad of the shining sapphire weather,
But we know more of it than they,
 Pain and I together.

They are the runners in the sun,
 Breathless and blinded by the race,
But we are watchers in the shade
 Who speak with Wonder face to face.

Sara Teasdale (1884–1933)

'Gently they go, the beautiful, the tender, the kind'

**Dirge Without Music**
Edna St. Vincent Millay

# Give me no counsel

From *Much Ado about Nothing*, Act V, Scene i

LEONATO
I pray thee, cease thy counsel,
Which falls into mine ears as profitless
As water in a sieve. Give not me counsel,
Nor let no comforter delight mine ear
But such a one whose wrongs do suit with mine.
Bring me a father that so loved his child,
Whose joy of her is overwhelmed like mine,
And bid him speak of patience.
Measure his woe the length and breadth of mine,
And let it answer every strain for strain,
As thus for thus, and such a grief for such,
In every lineament, branch, shape, and form.
If such a one will smile and stroke his beard,
Bid sorrow wag, cry 'hem' when he should groan,
Patch grief with proverbs, make misfortune drunk

With candle-wasters, bring him yet to me,
And I of him will gather patience.
But there is no such man. For, brother, men
Can counsel and speak comfort to that grief
Which they themselves not feel, but tasting it,
Their counsel turns to passion, which before
Would give preceptial med'cine to rage,
Fetter strong madness in a silken thread,
Charm ache with air and agony with words.
No, no, 'tis all men's office to speak patience
To those that wring under the load of sorrow,
But no man's virtue nor sufficiency
To be so moral when he shall endure
The like himself. Therefore give me no counsel.
My griefs cry louder than advertisement.

William Shakespeare (1564-1616)

# If I can stop one heart from breaking

If I can stop one heart from breaking,
I shall not live in vain;
If I can ease one life the aching,
Or cool one pain,
Or help one fainting robin
Unto his nest again,
I shall not live in vain.

Emily Dickinson (1830–1886)

'I count
my good
hours and
they guide
me well'

I count the moments of my mercies up
Elizabeth Jennings

# Time Long Past

Like the ghost of a dear friend dead
　　　　Is time long past.
A tone which is now forever fled,
A hope which is now forever past,
A love so sweet it could not last,
　　　　Was time long past.

There were sweet dreams in the night
　　　　Of time long past:
And, was it sadness or delight,
Each day a shadow onward cast
Which made us wish it yet might last –
　　　　That time long past.

There is regret, almost remorse,
　　　　For time long past.
'Tis like a child's belovèd corse
A father watches, till at last
Beauty is like remembrance, cast
　　　　From time long past.

Percy Bysshe Shelley (1792–1822)

# Reciprocity

I do not think that skies and meadows are
Moral, or that the fixture of a star
Comes of a quiet spirit, or that trees
Have wisdom in their windless silences.
Yet these are things invested in my mood
With constancy, and peace, and fortitude,
That in my troubled season I can cry
Upon the wide composure of the sky,
And envy fields, and wish that I might be
As little daunted as a star or tree.

John Drinkwater (1882–1937)

# On the Death of the Beloved

Though we need to weep your loss,
You dwell in that safe place in our hearts,
Where no storm or night or pain can reach you.

Your love was like the dawn
Brightening over our lives
Awakening beneath the dark
A further adventure of colour.

The sound of your voice
Found for us
A new music
That brightened everything.

Whatever you enfolded in your gaze
Quickened in the joy of its being;
You placed smiles like flowers
On the altar of the heart.
Your mind always sparkled
With wonder at things.

Though your days here were brief,
Your spirit was live, awake, complete.

We look towards each other no longer
From the old distance of our names;
Now you dwell inside the rhythm of breath,
As close to us as we are to ourselves.

Though we cannot see you with outward eyes,
We know our soul's gaze is upon your face,
Smiling back at us from within everything
To which we bring our best refinement.

Let us not look for you only in memory,
Where we would grow lonely without you.
You would want us to find you in presence,
Beside us when beauty brightens,
When kindness glows
And music echoes eternal tones.

When orchids brighten the earth,
Darkest winter has turned to spring;
May this dark grief flower with hope
In every heart that loves you.

May you continue to inspire us:

To enter each day with a generous heart.
To serve the call of courage and love
Until we see your beautiful face again
In that land where there is no more separation,
Where all tears will be wiped from our mind,
And where we will never lose you again.

John O'Donohue (1956 2008)

'I weep
like a
child for
the past'

**Piano**
D. H. Lawrence

# The End

Throughout the echoing chambers of my brain
    I hear your words in mournful cadence toll
    Like some slow passing-bell which warns the soul
Of sundering darkness. Unrelenting, fain
To batter down resistance, fall again
    Stroke after stroke, insistent diastole,
    The bitter blows of truth, until the whole
Is hammered into fact made strangely plain.
    Where shall I look for comfort? Not to you.
    Our worlds are drawn apart, our spirit's suns
Divided, and the light of mine burnt dim.
    Now in the haunted twilight I must do
    Your will. I grasp the cup which over-runs,
And with my trembling lips I touch the rim.

Amy Lowell (1874–1925)

# Oft, in the stilly night

Oft, in the stilly night,
 Ere slumber's chain has bound me,
Fond Memory brings the light
 Of other days around me;
  The smiles, the tears,
  Of boyhood's years,
 The words of love then spoken;
  The eyes that shone,
  Now dimmed and gone,
 The cheerful hearts now broken!
Thus, in the stilly night,
 Ere Slumber's chain hath bound me,
Sad Memory brings the light
 Of other days around me.

When I remember all
    The friends, so linked together,
I've seen around me fall,
    Like leaves in wintry weather;
        I feel like one
        Who treads alone
    Some banquet-hall deserted,
        Whose lights are fled,
        Whose garlands dead,
    And all but he departed!
Thus, in the stilly night,
    Ere Slumber's chain has bound me,
Sad Memory brings the light
    Of other days around me.

Thomas Moore (1779–1852)

# Warm summer sun
### Adapted from Robert Richardson's poem 'Annette'

Warm summer sun,
    Shine kindly here,
Warm southern wind,
    Blow softly here.
Green sod above,
    Lie light, lie light.
Good night, dear heart,
    Good night, good night.

Mark Twain (1835–1910)

# Mama never forgets her birds

Mama never forgets her birds,
Though in another tree –
She looks down just as often
And just as tenderly
As when her little mortal nest
With cunning care she wove –
If either of her 'sparrows fall,'
She 'notices,' above.

Emily Dickinson (1830–1886)

# On the Dunes

If there is any life when death is over,
    These tawny beaches will know much of me,
I shall come back, as constant and as changeful
    As the unchanging, many-colored sea.

If life was small, if it has made me scornful,
    Forgive me; I shall straighten like a flame
In the great calm of death, and if you want me
    Stand on the sea-ward dunes and call my name.

Sara Teasdale (1884-1933)

# The Flower
## Lines 1-14

    How fresh, oh Lord, how sweet and clean
Are thy returns! even as the flowers in spring;
    To which, besides their own demean,
The late-past frosts tributes of pleasure bring.
        Grief melts away
        Like snow in May,
    As if there were no such cold thing.

    Who would have thought my shriveled heart
Could have recovered greenness? It was gone
    Quite under ground; as flowers depart
To see their mother-root, when they have blown;
        Where they together
        All the hard weather,
    Dead to the world, keep house unknown.

George Herbert (1593-1633)

# From the pale and the deep

From the pale and the deep
    From the dark and bright –
From the violets that sleep –
    Away from light: –
From the lily that flashes
    At morn's glad call –
The bee gathers honey
    And sweets from all. –

There are hearts like bees
    In a world such as this,
That are given to please
    Through sorrow and bliss: –
Be the heaven of life
    As dark as it will –
Amid pleasure and strife
    They are smiling still.

They've a tear for the sad, –
    But there's balm in their sigh, –
And they laugh with the glad
    In sunshine and joy: –
They give hope to the gloom
    Of the mourner's thrall –
Like the bee they find honey
    And sweets in all.

Edward Lear (1812–1888)

# Life's uncertain voyage
From *Timon of Athens*, Act V, Scene i

TIMON
…tell them that, to ease them of their griefs,
Their fears of hostile strokes, their aches, losses,
Their pangs of love, with other incident throes
That nature's fragile vessel doth sustain
In life's uncertain voyage, I will some kindness do
  them.

William Shakespeare (1564–1616)

# No worst, there is none.
# Pitched past pitch of grief

No worst, there is none. Pitched past pitch of grief,
More pangs will, schooled at forepangs, wilder wring.
Comforter, where, where is your comforting?
Mary, mother of us, where is your relief?
My cries heave, herds-long; huddle in a main, a chief
Woe, wórld-sorrow; on an áge-old ánvil wince and
  sing –
Then lull, then leave off. Fury had shrieked 'No ling-
ering! Let me be fell: force I must be brief.'

O the mind, mind has mountains; cliffs of fall
Frightful, sheer, no-man-fathomed. Hold them cheap
May who ne'er hung there. Nor does long our small
Durance deal with that steep or deep. Here! creep,
Wretch, under a comfort serves in a whirlwind: all
Life death does end and each day dies with sleep.

Gerard Manley Hopkins (1844-1889)

# Chinese Poet Among Barbarians

The rain drives, drives endlessly,
Heavy threads of rain;
The wind beats at the shutters,
The surf drums on the shore;
Drunken telegraph poles lean sideways;
Dank summer cottages gloom hopelessly;
Bleak factory-chimneys are etched on the filmy
    distance,
Tepid with rain.
It seems I have lived for a hundred years
Among these things;
And it is useless for me now to make complaint
    against them.
For I know I shall never escape from this dull
    barbarian country,
Where there is none now left to lift a cool jade
    winecup,
Or share with me a single human thought.

John Gould Fletcher (1886-1950)

# From One Who Stays

How empty seems the town now you are gone!
    A wilderness of sad streets, where gaunt walls
    Hide nothing to desire; sunshine falls
Eery, distorted, as it long had shone
On white, dead faces tombed in halls of stone.
    The whir of motors, stricken through with calls
    Of playing boys, floats up at intervals;
But all these noises blur to one long moan.

    What quest is worth pursuing? And how strange
That other men still go accustomed ways!
I hate their interest in the things they do.
    A spectre-horde repeating without change
An old routine. Alone I know the days
Are still-born, and the world stopped, lacking you.

Amy Lowell (1874-1925)

# I Shall Return

I shall return again; I shall return
To laugh and love and watch with wonder-eyes
At golden noon the forest fires burn,
Wafting their blue-black smoke to sapphire skies.
I shall return to loiter by the streams
That bathe the brown blades of the bending grasses,
And realize once more my thousand dreams
Of waters rushing down the mountain passes.
I shall return to hear the fiddle and fife
Of village dances, dear delicious tunes
That stir the hidden depths of native life,
Stray melodies of dim remembered runes.
I shall return, I shall return again,
To ease my mind of long, long years of pain.

Claude McKay (1889-1948)

# Grief Thief of Time

Grief thief of time crawls off,
The moon-drawn grave, with the seafaring years,
The knave of pain steals off
The sea-halved faith that blew time to his knees,
The old forget the cries,
Lean time on tide and times the wind stood rough,
Call back the castaways
Riding the sea light on a sunken path,
The old forget the grief,
Hack of the cough, the hanging albatross,
Cast back the bone of youth
And salt-eyed stumble bedward where she lies
Who tossed the high tide in a time of stories
And timelessly lies loving with the thief.

Now Jack my fathers let the time-faced crook,
Death flashing from his sleeve,
With swag of bubbles in a seedy sack
Sneak down the stallion grave,
Bull's-eye the outlaw through a eunuch crack
And free the twin-boxed grief,
No silver whistles chase him down the weeks'
Dayed peaks to day to death,
These stolen bubbles have the bites of snakes
And the undead eye-teeth,
No third eye probe into a rainbow's sex
That bridged the human halves,
All shall remain and on the graveward gulf
Shape with my fathers' thieves.

Dylan Thomas (1914–1953)

# Just Whistle a Bit

Just whistle a bit, if the day be dark,
 And the sky be overcast:
If mute be the voice of the piping lark,
 Why, pipe your own small blast.

And it's wonderful how o'er the gray sky – track
 The truant warbler comes stealing back.
But why need he come? for your soul's at rest,
 And the song in the heart, – ah, that is best.

Just whistle a bit, if the night be drear
 And the stars refuse to shine:
And a gleam that mocks the starlight clear
 Within you glows benign.

Till the dearth of light in the glooming skies
 Is lost to the sight of your soul-lit eyes.
What matters the absence of moon or star?
 The light within is the best by far.

Just whistle a bit, if there's work to do,
 With the mind or in the soil.
And your note will turn out a talisman true
 To exorcise grim Toil.

It will lighten your burden and make you feel
    That there's nothing like work as a sauce for a meal.
And with song in your heart and the meal in – its place,
    There'll be joy in your bosom and light in your face.

Just whistle a bit, if your heart be sore
    'Tis a wonderful balm for pain.
Just pipe some old melody o'er and o'er
    Till it soothes like summer rain.

And perhaps 'twould be best in a later day,
    When Death comes stalking down the way,
To knock at your bosom and see if you're fit,
    Then, as you wait calmly, just whistle a bit.

Paul Laurence Dunbar (1872–1906)

# We lack, yet cannot fix upon the lack

We lack, yet cannot fix upon the lack:
    Not this, nor that; yet somewhat, certainly.
    We see the things we do not yearn to see
Around us: and what see we glancing back?
Lost hopes that leave our hearts upon the rack,
    Hopes that were never ours yet seemed to be,
    For which we steered on life's salt stormy sea
Braving the sunstroke and the frozen pack.
If thus to look behind is all in vain,
    And all in vain to look to left or right,
Why face we not our future once again,
Launching with hardier hearts across the main,
    Straining dim eyes to catch the invisible sight,
And strong to bear ourselves in patient pain?

Christina Rossetti (1830-1894)

# My own heart let me more have pity on

My own heart let me more have pity on; let
Me live to my sad self hereafter kind,
Charitable; not live this tormented mind
With this tormented mind tormenting yet.
I cast for comfort I can no more get
By groping round my comfortless, than blind
Eyes in their dark can day or thirst can find
Thirst's all-in-all in all a world of wet.

Soul, self; come, poor Jackself, I do advise
You, jaded, lét be; call off thoughts awhile
Elsewhere; leave comfort root-room; let joy size
At God knows when to God knows what; whose
  smile
'S not wrung, see you; unforeseentimes rather –
  as skies
Betweenpie mountains – lights a lovely mile.

Gerard Manley Hopkins (1844-1889)

# Now I am a plant, a weed

Now I am a plant, a weed,
Bending and swinging
On a rocky ledge;
And now I am a long brown grass
Fluttering like flame;
I am a reed;
An old shell singing
For ever the same;
A drift of sedge;
A white, white stone;
A bone;
Until I pass
Into sand again,
And spin and blow
To and fro, to and fro,
On the edge of the sea
In the fading light –
For the light fades.

But if you were to come you would not say:
'She is not waiting here for me;
She has forgotten.' Have we not in play
Disguised ourselves as weed and stones and grass
While the strange ships did pass
Gently, gravely, leaving a curl of foam
That uncurled softly about our island home,
Bubbles of foam that glittered on the stone
Like rainbows? Look, darling! No, they are gone.
And the white sails have melted into the sailing sky ...

Katherine Mansfield (1888–1923)

'find
strength
in what
remains
behind'

**Splendor in the Grass**
William Wordsworth

# I can wade grief

I can wade grief –
Whole pools of it –
I'm used to that.
But the least push of joy
Breaks up my feet,
And I tip – drunken.
Let no pebble smile,
'Twas the new liquor, –
That was all!

Power is only pain –
Stranded, through discipline,
Till weights will hang.
Give balm to giants,
And they'll wilt, like men.
Give Himmaleh, –
They'll carry him!

Emily Dickinson (1830-1886)

# He would not stay for me, and who can wonder

He would not stay for me, and who can wonder?
    He would not stay for me to stand and gaze.
I shook his hand, and tore my heart in sunder,
    And went with half my life about my ways.

A. E. Housman (1859–1936)

# The Heart of the Wood

My hope and my love,
we will go for a while into the wood,
scattering the dew,
where we will see the trout,
we will see the blackbird on its nest;
the deer and the buck calling,
the little bird that is sweetest singing on the branches;
the cuckoo on the top of the fresh green;
and death will never come near us for ever in the
  sweet wood.

Translated from the Gaelic by Lady Augusta Gregory
(1852-1932)

# The Storm

If as the windes and waters here below
                              Do flie and flow,
My sighs and tears as busie were above;
                              Sure they would move
And much affect thee, as tempestuous times
Amaze poore mortals, and object their crimes.

Starres have their storms, ev'n in a high degree,
                              As well as we.
A throbbing conscience spurred by remorse
                              Hath a strange force:
It quits the earth, and mounting more and more
Dares to assault thee, and besiege thy doore.

There it stands knocking, to thy musicks wrong,
                              And drowns the song.
Glorie and honour are set by, till it
                              An answer get.
Poets have wrong'd poore storms: such dayes are best;
They purge the aire without, within the breast.

George Herbert (1593–1633)

# And the goddesses thronged about her

## From *The Iliad,* Book XVIII: 'Tidings of the death of Patroclus reach his friend Achilles'

… a black cloud of grief enwrapped Achilles, and with both his hands he took the dark dust and strewed it over his head and defiled his fair face, and on his fragrant tunic the black ashes fell. And himself in the dust lay outstretched, mighty in his mightiness, and with his own hands he tore and marred his hair.

Then terribly did Achilles groan aloud, and his queenly mother heard him as she sat in the depths of the sea beside the old man her father. Thereat she uttered a shrill cry, and the goddesses thronged about her, even all the daughters of Nereus that were in the deep of the sea.

Homer (8th century BCE)
Translated from the Greek by A. T. Murray

# Songs

I love the dear old ballads best,
      That tell of love and death,
Whose every line sings love's unrest
      Or mourns the parting breath.
I love those songs the heart can feel,
      That make our pulses throb;
When lovers plead or contrites kneel
      With choking sigh and sob.

God sings through songs that touch the heart,
      And none are prized save these.
Though men may ply their gilded art
      For fortune, fame, or fees,
The muse that sets the songster's soul
      Ablaze with lyric fire,
Holds nature up, an open scroll,
      And builds art's funeral pyre.

Paul Laurence Dunbar (1872-1906)

'Move
back and
forth
into the
change'

**Let This Darkness Be a Bell Tower**
Rainer Maria Rilke

# The Unquiet Grave
*A ballad*

### I

'The wind doth blow to-day, my love,
    And a few small drops of rain,
I never had but one true-love,
    In cold grave she was lain.

### II

'I'll do as much for my true-love
    As any young man may,
I'll sit and mourn all at her grave
    For a twelvemonth and a day.'

### III

The twelvemonth and a day being up,
    The dead began to speak
'Oh who sits weeping on my grave,
    And will not let me sleep?' –

### IV

''Tis I, my love, sits on your grave,
    And will not let you sleep,
For I crave one kiss of your clay-cold lips,
    And that is all I seek.' –

## V

'You crave one kiss of my clay-cold lips,
  But my breath smells earthy strong,
If you have one kiss of my clay-cold lips,
  Your time will not be long.

## VI

''Tis down in yonder garden green,
  Love, where we used to walk,
The finest flower that ere was seen
  Is wither'd to a stalk.

## VII

'The stalk is wither'd dry, my love,
  So will our hearts decay;
So make yourself content, my love,
  Till God calls you away.'

Anon

# When I am dead, my dearest

When I am dead, my dearest,
    Sing no sad songs for me;
Plant thou no roses at my head,
    Nor shady cypress tree:
Be the green grass above me
    With showers and dewdrops wet;
And if thou wilt, remember,
    And if thou wilt, forget.

I shall not see the shadows,
    I shall not feel the rain;
I shall not hear the nightingale
    Sing on, as if in pain:
And dreaming through the twilight
    That doth not rise nor set,
Haply I may remember,
    And haply may forget.

Christina Rossetti (1830–1894)

# Surprised by Joy

Surprised by joy – impatient as the Wind
I turned to share the transport – Oh! with whom
But Thee, long buried in the silent Tomb,
That spot which no vicissitude can find?
Love, faithful love, recalled thee to my mind –
But how could I forget thee? Through what power,
Even for the least division of an hour,
Have I been so beguiled as to be blind
To my most grievous loss? – That thought's return
Was the worst pang that sorrow ever bore,
Save one, one only, when I stood forlorn,
Knowing my heart's best treasure was no more;
That neither present time, nor years unborn
Could to my sight that heavenly face restore.

William Wordsworth (1770-1850)

# Everything Is Going to Be All Right

How should I not be glad to contemplate
the clouds clearing beyond the dormer window
and a high tide reflected on the ceiling?
There will be dying, there will be dying,
but there is no need to go into that.
The lines flow from the hand unbidden
and the hidden source is the watchful heart;
the sun rises in spite of everything
and the far cities are beautiful and bright.
I lie here in a riot of sunlight
watching the day break and the clouds flying.
Everything is going to be all right.

Derek Mahon (1941-2020)

'Give sorrow words'

**Macbeth, Act IV, Scene iii**
William Shakespeare

# Interim

## Lines 17–102

You are not here. I know that you are gone,
And will not ever enter here again.
And yet it seems to me, if I should speak,
Your silent step must wake across the hall;
If I should turn my head, that your sweet eyes
Would kiss me from the door. – So short a time
To teach my life its transposition to
This difficult and unaccustomed key! –
The room is as you left it; your last touch –
A thoughtless pressure, knowing not itself
As saintly – hallows now each simple thing;
Hallows and glorifies, and glows between
The dust's grey fingers like a shielded light.

There is your book, just as you laid it down,
Face to the table, – I cannot believe
That you are gone! – Just then it seemed to me
You must be here. I almost laughed to think
How like reality the dream had been;
Yet knew before I laughed, and so was still.
That book, outspread, just as you laid it down!
Perhaps you thought, 'I wonder what comes next,
And whether this or this will be the end';
So rose, and left it, thinking to return.

Perhaps that chair, when you arose and passed
Out of the room, rocked silently a while
Ere it again was still. When you were gone
Forever from the room, perhaps that chair,
Stirred by your movement, rocked a little while,
Silently, to and fro …

And here are the last words your fingers wrote,
Scrawled in broad characters across a page
In this brown book I gave you. Here your hand,
Guiding your rapid pen, moved up and down.
Here with a looping knot you crossed a 't,'
And here another like it, just beyond
These two eccentric 'e's.' You were so small,
And wrote so brave a hand!
                                How strange it seems
That of all words these are the words you chose!
And yet a simple choice; you did not know
You would not write again. If you had known –
But then, it does not matter, – and indeed
If you had known there was so little time
You would have dropped your pen and come to me
And this page would be empty, and some phrase
Other than this would hold my wonder now.

Yet, since you could not know, and it befell
That these are the last words your fingers wrote,
There is a dignity some might not see
In this, 'I picked the first sweet-pea to-day.'
To-day! Was there an opening bud beside it
You left until to-morrow? – O my love,
The things that withered, – and you came not back!
That day you filled this circle of my arms
That now is empty. (O my empty life!)
That day – that day you picked the first sweet-pea, –
And brought it in to show me! I recall
With terrible distinctness how the smell
Of your cool gardens drifted in with you.
I know, you held it up for me to see
And flushed because I looked not at the flower,
But at your face; and when behind my look
You saw such unmistakable intent
You laughed and brushed your flower against my
  lips.
(You were the fairest thing God ever made,
I think.) And then your hands above my heart
Drew down its stem into a fastening,
And while your head was bent I kissed your hair.
I wonder if you knew. (Beloved hands!

Somehow I cannot seem to see them still.
Somehow I cannot seem to see the dust
In your bright hair.) What is the need of Heaven
When earth can be so sweet? – If only God
Had let us love, – and show the world the way!
Strange cancellings must ink th' eternal books
When love-crossed-out will bring the answer right!
That first sweet-pea! I wonder where it is.
It seems to me I laid it down somewhere,
And yet, – I am not sure. I am not sure,
Even, if it was white or pink; for then
'Twas much like any other flower to me,
Save that it was the first. I did not know,
Then, that it was the last. If I had known –
But then, it does not matter. Strange how few,
After all's said and done, the things that are
Of moment.

Edna St. Vincent Millay (1892 –1950)

'I am thankful for my bit of sky'

**Solace**
Clarissa Scott Delany

# A Modest Love

The lowest trees have tops, the ant her gall,
    The fly her spleen, the little sparks their heat;
The slender hairs cast shadows, though but small,
    And bees have stings, although they be not great;
Seas have their source, and so have shallow springs;
And love is love, in beggars as in kings.

Where rivers smoothest run, deep are the fords;
    The dial stirs, yet none perceives it move;
The firmest faith is in the fewest words;
    The turtles cannot sing, and yet they love:
True hearts have eyes and ears, no tongues to speak;
They hear and see, and sigh, and then they break.

Sir Edward Dyer (1543-1607)

# Spring in War-Time

I feel the spring far off, far off,
    The faint, far scent of bud and leaf –
Oh, how can spring take heart to come
    To a world in grief,
        Deep grief?

The sun turns north, the days grow long,
    Later the evening star grows bright –
How can the daylight linger on
    For men to fight,
        Still fight?

The grass is waking in the ground,
    Soon it will rise and blow in waves –
How can it have the heart to sway
    Over the graves,
        New graves?

Under the boughs where lovers walked
    The apple-blooms will shed their breath –
But what of all the lovers now
    Parted by Death,
        Gray Death?

Sara Teasdale (1884–1933)

# The Window

Your body is away from me
but there is a window open
from my heart to yours.
From this window, like the moon
I keep sending news secretly.

Rumi (1207–1273)

# On Another's Sorrow

Can I see another's woe,
And not be in sorrow too?
Can I see another's grief,
And not seek for kind relief?

Can I see a falling tear,
And not feel my sorrow's share?
Can a father see his child
Weep, nor be with sorrow filled?

Can a mother sit and hear
An infant groan, an infant fear?
No, no, never can it be!
Never, never can it be.

And can he who smiles on all
Hear the wren with sorrows small,
Hear the small bird's grief and care,
Hear the woes that infants bear,

And not sit beside the nest,
Pouring pity in their breast;
And not sit the cradle near,
Weeping tear on infant's tear?

And not sit both night and day,
Wiping all our tears away?
O no! never can it be,
Never, never can it be.

He doth give his joy to all:
He becomes an infant small,
He becomes a man of woe,
He doth feel the sorrow too.

Think not thou canst sigh a sigh,
And thy Maker is not by:
Think not thou canst weep a tear,
And thy Maker is not near.

O! he gives to us his joy,
That our grief he may destroy:
Till our grief is fled and gone
He doth sit by us and moan.

**William Blake** (1757–1827)

# They who are near me do not know

They who are near me do not know that you are
  nearer to me than they are.
Those who speak to me do not know that my heart
  is full with your unspoken words.
Those who crowd in my path do not know that I am
  walking alone with you.
Those who love me do not know that their love
  brings you to my heart.

Rabindranath Tagore (1861–1941)

# Do not stand at my grave and weep

Do not stand at my grave and weep
I am not there. I do not sleep.

I am a thousand winds that blow.
I am the diamond glints on snow.
I am the sunlight on ripened grain.
I am the gentle autumn rain.

When you awaken in the morning's hush
I am the swift uplifting rush
Of quiet birds in circled flight.
I am the soft stars that shine at night.

Do not stand at my grave and cry;
I am not there. I did not die.

Anon

# The Instinct of Hope

Is there another world for this frail dust
To warm with life and be itself again?
Something about me daily speaks there must,
And why should instinct nourish hopes in vain?
'Tis nature's prophesy that such will be,
And everything seems struggling to explain
The close sealed volume of its mystery.
Time wandering onward keeps its usual pace
As seeming anxious of eternity,
To meet that calm and find a resting place.
E'en the small violet feels a future power
And waits each year renewing blooms to bring,
And surely man is no inferior flower
To die unworthy of a second spring?

John Clare (1793-1864)

# On Pain

And a woman spoke, saying, Tell us of Pain.
And he said:
Your pain is the breaking of the shell that encloses
   your understanding.
Even as the stone of the fruit must break, that its
   heart may stand in the sun, so must you know pain.
And could you keep your heart in wonder at the daily
   miracles of your life, your pain would not seem less
   wondrous than your joy;
And you would accept the seasons of your heart,
   even as you have always accepted the seasons that
   pass over your fields.
And you would watch with serenity through the
   winters of your grief.
Much of your pain is self-chosen.
It is the bitter potion by which the physician within
   you heals your sick self.
Therefore trust the physician, and drink his remedy
   in silence and tranquillity:
For his hand, though heavy and hard, is guided by
   the tender hand of the Unseen,
And the cup he brings, though it burn your lips, has
   been fashioned of the clay which the Potter has
   moistened with His own sacred tears.

Kahlil Gibran (1883–1931)

# To every thing there is a season
### King James Bible, Ecclesiastes 3, verses 1–8

To every thing there is a season, and a time to every
purpose under the heaven:

A time to be born, and a time to die; a time to plant,
and a time to pluck up that which is planted;

A time to kill, and a time to heal; a time to break
down, and a time to build up;

A time to weep, and a time to laugh; a time to
mourn, and a time to dance;

A time to cast away stones, and a time to gather
stones together; a time to embrace, and a time to
refrain from embracing;

A time to get, and a time to lose; a time to keep, and
a time to cast away;

A time to rend, and a time to sew; a time to keep
silence, and a time to speak;

A time to love, and a time to hate; a time of war, and
a time of peace.

'Be and
be better.
For they
existed'

Ailey, Baldwin, Floyd, Killens,
and Mayfield
Maya Angelou

# Pushing Through

It's possible I am pushing through solid rock
in flintlike layers, as the ore lies, alone;
I am such a long way in I see no way through,
and no space: everything is close to my face,
and everything close to my face is stone.

I don't have much knowledge yet in grief –
so this massive darkness makes me small.
*You* be the master: make yourself fierce, break in:
then your great transforming will happen to me,
and my great grief cry will happen to you.

Rainer Maria Rilke (1875–1926)
Translated from the German by Robert Bly

# Credo

I cannot find my way: there is no star
In all the shrouded heavens anywhere;
And there is not a whisper in the air
Of any living voice but one so far
That I can hear it only as a bar
Of lost, imperial music, played when fair
And angel fingers wove, and unaware,
Dead leaves to garlands where no roses are.

No, there is not a glimmer, nor a call,
For one that welcomes, welcomes when he fears,
The black and awful chaos of the night;
For through it all – above, beyond it all –
I know the far-sent message of the years,
I feel the coming glory of the Light.

Edwin Arlington Robinson (1869–1935)

# Splendor in the Grass

From *Ode: Intimations of Immortality from Recollections of Early Childhood*

What though the radiance which was once so bright
Be now forever taken from my sight,
    Though nothing can bring back the hour
Of splendor in the grass, of glory in the flower;
    We will grieve not, rather find
    Strength in what remains behind;
    In the primal sympathy
    Which, having been, must ever be;
    In the soothing thoughts that spring
    Out of human suffering;
    In the faith that looks through death,
In years that bring the philosophic mind.

William Wordsworth (1770–1850)

# Sonnet 30

When to the sessions of sweet silent thought
I summon up remembrance of things past,
I sigh the lack of many a thing I sought,
And with old woes new wail my dear time's waste:
Then can I drown an eye, unused to flow,
For precious friends hid in death's dateless night,
And weep afresh love's long since cancelled woe,
And moan th' expense of many a vanished sight;
Then can I grieve at grievances foregone,
And heavily from woe to woe tell o'er
The sad account of fore-bemoanèd moan,
Which I new pay as if not paid before.
　　But if the while I think on thee, dear friend,
　　All losses are restored, and sorrows end.

William Shakespeare (1564-1616)

# Twelve Songs: IX

Stop all the clocks, cut off the telephone,
Prevent the dog from barking with a juicy bone,
Silence the pianos and with muffled drum
Bring out the coffin, let the mourners come.

Let aeroplanes circle moaning overhead
Scribbling on the sky the message He Is Dead
Put crêpe bows round the white necks of the public
  doves,
Let the traffic policemen wear black cotton gloves.

He was my North, my South, my East and West,
My working week and my Sunday rest,
My noon, my midnight, my talk, my song;
I thought that love would last for ever: I was wrong.

The stars are not wanted now: put out every one;
Pack up the moon and dismantle the sun;
Pour away the ocean and sweep up the wood.
For nothing now can ever come to any good.

W. H. Auden (1907–1973)

# Piano

Softly, in the dusk, a woman is singing to me;
Taking me back down the vista of years, till I see
A child sitting under the piano, in the boom of the
  tingling strings
And pressing the small, poised feet of a mother who
  smiles as she sings.

In spite of myself, the insidious mastery of song
Betrays me back, till the heart of me weeps to belong
To the old Sunday evenings at home, with winter
  outside
And hymns in the cosy parlour, the tinkling piano
  our guide.

So now it is vain for the singer to burst into clamour
With the great black piano appassionato. The
  glamour
Of childish days is upon me, my manhood is cast
Down in the flood of remembrance, I weep like a
  child for the past.

D. H. Lawrence (1885–1930)

# A hunger seized my heart
## Canto XCV, *In Memoriam A. H. H.*

A hunger seized my heart; I read
    Of that glad year which once had been,
    In those fall'n leaves which kept their green,
The noble letters of the dead:

And strangely on the silence broke
    The silent-speaking words, and strange
    Was love's dumb cry defying change
To test his worth; and strangely spoke

The faith, the vigour, bold to dwell
    On doubts that drive the coward back,
    And keen thro' wordy snares to track
Suggestion to her inmost cell.

So word by word, and line by line,
    The dead man touch'd me from the past,
    And all at once it seem'd at last
The living soul was flash'd on mine,

And mine in this was wound, and whirl'd
    About empyreal heights of thought,
    And came on that which is, and caught
The deep pulsations of the world,

Æonian music measuring out
    The steps of Time – the shocks of Chance –
    The blows of Death. At length my trance
Was cancell'd, stricken thro' with doubt.

Vague words! but ah, how hard to frame
    In matter-moulded forms of speech,
    Or ev'n for intellect to reach
Thro' memory that which I became:

Till now the doubtful dusk reveal'd
    The knolls once more where, couch'd at ease,
    The white kine glimmer'd, and the trees
Laid their dark arms about the field:

And suck'd from out the distant gloom
    A breeze began to tremble o'er
    The large leaves of the sycamore,
And fluctuate all the still perfume,

And gathering freshlier overhead,
    Rock'd the full-foliaged elms, and swung
    The heavy-folded rose, and flung
The lilies to and fro, and said

'The dawn, the dawn,' and died away;
    And East and West, without a breath,
    Mixt their dim lights, like life and death,
To broaden into boundless day.

Lord Alfred Tennyson (1809–1892)

# I count the moments of my mercies up

I count the moments of my mercies up.
I make a list of love and find it full.
I do all this before I fall asleep.

Others examine consciences. I tell
My beads of gracious moments shining still.
I count my good hours and they guide me well

Into a sleepless night. It is when I fill
Pages with what I think I am made for,
A life writing poems. Then may they heal

The pain of silence for all those who stare
At stars as I do but are helpless to
Make the bright necklace. May I set ajar

The door of closed minds. Words come and words go
And poetry is pain as well as passion
But in the large flights of imagination

I see for one crammed second, order so
Explicit that I need no more persuasion.

Elizabeth Jennings (1926–2001)

# The Greatest of These is Charity

A moon impoverished amid stars curtailed,
    A sun of its exuberant lustre shorn,
    A transient morning that is scarcely morn,
A lingering night in double dimness veiled. —
Our hands are slackened and our strength has failed:
    We born to darkness, wherefore were we born?
    No ripening more for olive, grape, or corn:
Faith faints, hope faints, even love himself has paled.
Nay! love lifts up a face like any rose
    Flushing and sweet above a thorny stem,
Softly protesting that the way he knows;
    And as for faith and hope, will carry them
    Safe to the gate of New Jerusalem,
Where light shines full and where the palm-tree
    blows.

Christina Rossetti (1830–1894)

# In the Fields

Lord, when I look at lovely things which pass,
    Under old trees the shadow of young leaves
Dancing to please the wind along the grass,
    Or the gold stillness of the August sun on the
      August sheaves;
Can I believe there is a heavenlier world than this?
    And if there is
Will the strange heart of any everlasting thing
    Bring me these dreams that take my breath away?
They come at evening with the home-flying rooks
 and the scent of hay,
    Over the fields. They come in spring.

Charlotte Mew (1869–1928)

# The secret of bringing peace to a distraught soul

## Adapted from a letter sent to a friend in bereavement

It is only magicians who pretend
    to calm storms with words.

The would-be comforter inflames
and excites the wounds of the soul
or, at tempting to comfort,
moves to fresh tears:

but Time cures at last.

Nature never intended that our wounds
should be closed in a moment –
that we should pass in a second
from sickness to health:

but Time cures at last.

Voltaire (1694–1778)
Translated from the French by S. G. Tallentyre

# All things pass

All things pass

A sunrise does not last all morning

All things pass

A cloud burst does not last all day

All things pass

Nor a sunset all night

All things pass

What always changes?

Earth … Sky … thunder
Mountain … water
Wind … fire … lake …

.

These change

And if these do not last

Do man's visions last?
Do man's illusions?

During the session
Take things as they come

All things pass

Timothy Leary (1920-1996) after Lao Tzu (6th century BCE)

# Consolation

All are not taken; there are left behind
Living Beloveds, tender looks to bring
And make the daylight still a happy thing,
And tender voices, to make soft the wind:
But if it were not so – if I could find
No love in all this world for comforting,
Nor any path but hollowly did ring
Where 'dust to dust' the love from life disjoined;
And if, before those sepulchres unmoving
I stood alone (as some forsaken lamb
Goes bleating up the moors in weary dearth)
Crying 'Where are ye, O my loved and loving?' –
I know a Voice would sound, 'Daughter, I AM.
Can I suffice for HEAVEN and not for earth?'

Elizabeth Barrett Browning (1806-1861)

# Deer

Shy in their herding dwell the fallow deer.
They are spirits of wild sense. Nobody near
Comes upon their pastures. There a life they live,
Of sufficient beauty, phantom, fugitive,
Treading as in jungles free leopards do,
Printless as evelight, instant as dew.
The great kine are patient, and home-coming sheep
Know our bidding. The fallow deer keep
Delicate and far their counsels wild,
Never to be folded reconciled
To the spoiling hand as the poor flocks are;
Lightfoot, and swift, and unfamiliar,
These you may not hinder, unconfined
Beautiful flocks of the mind.

John Drinkwater (1882–1937)

# Talking to Grief

Ah, grief, I should not treat you
like a homeless dog
who comes to the back door
for a crust, for a meatless bone.
I should trust you.

I should coax you
into the house and give you
your own corner,
a worn mat to lie on,
your own water dish.

You think I don't know you've been living
under my porch.
You long for your real place to be readied
before winter comes. You need
your name,
your collar and tag. You need
the right to warn off intruders,
to consider
my house your own
and me your person
and yourself
my own dog.

Denise Levertov (1923-1997)

# Monody

To have known him, to have loved him
    After loneness long;
And then to be estranged in life,
    And neither in the wrong;
And now for death to set his seal –
    Ease me, a little ease, my song!

By wintry hills his hermit-mound
    The sheeted snow-drifts drape,
And houseless there the snow-bird flits
    Beneath the fir-trees' crape:
Glazed now with ice the cloistral vine
    That hid the shyest grape.

Herman Melville (1819–1891)

# Past Days

'Tis strange to think there *was* a time
When mirth was not an empty name,
When laughter really cheered the heart,
And frequent smiles unbidden came,
And tears of grief would only flow
In sympathy for others' woe;

When speech expressed the inward thought,
And heart to kindred heart was bare,
And Summer days were far too short
For all the pleasures crowded there;
And silence, solitude, and rest,
Now welcome to the weary breast –

Were all unprized, uncourted then –
And all the joy one spirit showed,
The other deeply felt again;
And friendship like a river flowed,
Constant and strong its silent course,
For nought withstood its gentle force:

When night, the holy time of peace,
Was dreaded as the parting hour;
When speech and mirth at once must cease,
And Silence must resume her power;
Though ever free from pains and woes,
She only brought us calm repose.

And when the blessed dawn again
Brought daylight to the blushing skies,
We woke, and not *reluctant* then,
To joyless *labour* did we rise;
But full of hope, and glad and gay,
We welcomed the returning day.

Anne Brontë (1820-1849)

# Canoe

Well, I am thinking this may be my last
summer, but cannot lose even a part
of pleasure in the old-fashioned art
of idleness. I cannot stand aghast

at whatever doom hovers in the background;
while grass and buildings and the somnolent river
who know they are allowed to last for ever
exchange between them the whole subdued sound

of this hot time. What sudden fearful fate
can deter my shade wandering next year
from a return? Whistle, and I will hear
and come another evening when this boat

travels with you alone towards Iffley:
as you lie looking up for thunder again,
this cool touch does not betoken rain;
it is my spirit that kisses your mouth lightly.

Keith Douglas (1920-1944)

# 'Now you dwell inside the rhythm of breath'

**On the Death of the Beloved**
John O'Donohue

# The Water of Eternal Life

Every form you see has its archetype in the placeless
  world;
If the form perished, no matter, since its Original is
  everlasting.
Every fair shape you have seen, every deep saying
  you have heard,
Be not cast down that it perished; for that is not so.
Whereas the Spring-head is undying, its branch gives
  water continually;
Since neither can cease, why are you lamenting?
Conceive the Soul as a fountain, and these created
  things as rivers:
While the Fountain flows, the rivers run from it.
Put grief out of your head and keep quaffing this
  River-water;
Do not think of the Water failing, for this Water is
  without end.

Rumi (1207-1273)
Translated by R. A. Nicholson

# Interim

The night was made for rest and sleep,
For winds that softly sigh;
It was not made for grief and tears;
So then why do I cry?

The wind that blows through leafy trees
Is soft and warm and sweet;
For me the night is a gracious cloak
To hide my soul's defeat.

Just one dark hour of shaken depths,
Of bitter black despair –
Another day will find me brave,
And not afraid to dare.

Clarissa Scott Delany (1901-1927)

# The Harp of Broken Strings

A stranger in a stranger land,
    Too calm to weep, too sad to smile,
I take my harp of broken strings,
    A weary moment to beguile;
And tho' no hope its promise brings,
    And present joy is not for me,
Still o'er that harp I love to bend,
    And feel its broken melody
With all my shattered feelings blend.

I love to hear its funeral voice
    Proclaim how sad my lot, how lone;
And when, my spirit wilder grows,
    To list its deeper, darker tone.
And when my soul more madly glows
    Above the wrecks that round it lie,
It fills me with a strange delight,
    Past mortal bearing, proud and high,
To feel its music swell to might.

When beats my heart in doubt and awe,
    And Reason pales upon her throne,
Ah, then, when no kind voice can cheer
    The lot too desolate, too lone,
Its tones come sweet upon my ear,
    As twilight o'er some landscape fair:
As light upon the wings of night

(The meteor flashes in the air,
The rising stars) its tones are bright.

And now by Sacramento's stream,
    What mem'ries sweet its music brings –
The vows of love, its smiles and tears,
    Hang o'er this harp of broken strings.
It speaks, and midst her blushing fears
    The beauteous one before me stands!
Pure spirit in her downcast eyes,
    And like twin doves her folded hands!

It breathes again – and at my side
    She kneels, with grace divinely rare –
Then showering kisses on my lips,
    She hides our blisses with her hair;
Then trembling with delight, she flings
    Her beauteous self into my arms,
As if o'erpowered, she sought for wings
    To hide her from her conscious charms!

It breathes once more, and bowed in grief,
    The bloom has left her cheek forever,
While, like my broken harp-strings now,
    Behold her form with feeling quiver!
She turns her face o'errun with tears,
    To him that silent bends above her,

And, by the sweets of other years,
    Entreats him still, oh, still to love her!

He loves her still – but darkness falls
    Upon his ruined fortunes now,
And 't is his exile doom to flee.
    The dews, like death, are on his brow,
And cold the pang about his heart
    Oh, cease – to die is agony:
'T is more than death when loved ones part!

Well may this harp of broken strings
    Seem sweet to me by this lonely shore.
When like a spirit it breaks forth,
    And speaks of beauty evermore!
When like a spirit it evokes
    The buried joys of early youth,
And clothes the shrines of early love,
    With all the radiant light of truth!

John Rollin Ridge (1827–1867)

# Dirge Without Music

I am not resigned to the shutting away of loving
  hearts in the hard ground.
So it is, and so it will be, for so it has been, time out
  of mind:
Into the darkness they go, the wise and the lovely.
  Crowned
With lilies and with laurel they go; but I am not
  resigned.

Lovers and thinkers, into the earth with you.
Be one with the dull, the indiscriminate dust.
A fragment of what you felt, of what you knew,
A formula, a phrase remains, – but the best is lost.

The answers quick and keen, the honest look, the
  laughter, the love, –
They are gone. They are gone to feed the roses.
  Elegant and curled
Is the blossom. Fragrant is the blossom. I know.
  But I do not approve.
More precious was the light in your eyes than all the
  roses in the world.

Down, down, down into the darkness of the grave
Gently they go, the beautiful, the tender, the kind;
Quietly they go, the intelligent, the witty, the brave.
I know. But I do not approve. And I am not resigned.

Edna St. Vincent Millay (1892–1950)

# Everyone Sang

Everyone suddenly burst out singing;
And I was filled with such delight
As prisoned birds must find in freedom,
Winging wildly across the white
Orchards and dark-green fields; on – on – and out of
  sight.

Everyone's voice was suddenly lifted;
And beauty came like the setting sun:
My heart was shaken with tears; and horror
Drifted away ... O, but Everyone
Was a bird; and the song was wordless; the singing
  will never be done.

Siegfried Sassoon (1886–1967)

# There is a pleasure in the pathless woods

From *Childe Harold's Pilgrimage*

There is a pleasure in the pathless woods,
There is a rapture on the lonely shore,
There is society, where none intrudes,
By the deep Sea, and music in its roar:
I love not Man the less, but Nature more,
From these our interviews, in which I steal
From all I may be, or have been before,
To mingle with the Universe, and feel
What I can ne'er express, yet cannot all conceal.

Lord Byron (1788-1824)

# Consolation

Though he that ever kind and true
Kept stoutly step by step with you
Your whole long gusty lifetime through,
Be gone a while before,
Be now a moment gone before,
Yet, doubt not, soon the seasons shall restore
Your friend to you.

He has but turned the corner. Still
He pushes on with right good will,
Through mire and marsh, by heugh and hill,
That self-same arduous way –
That self-same upland, hopeful way,
That you and he through many a doubtful day
Attempted still.

He is not dead, this friend – not dead,
But in the path we mortals tread
Got some few trifling steps ahead
And nearer to the end;
So that you too, once past the bend,
Shall meet again, as face to face, this friend
You fancy dead.

Push gaily on, strong heart! The while
You travel forward mile by mile,
He loiters with a backward smile
Till you can overtake,
And strains his eyes to search his wake,
Or whistling, as he sees you through the brake,
Waits on a stile.

Robert Louis Stevenson (1850–1894)

# To weep is to make less the depth of grief
From *Henry VI Part 3*, Act II, Scene i

EDWARD

Sweet Duke of York, our prop to lean upon,
Now thou art gone, we have no staff, no stay.
O Clifford, boist'rous Clifford, thou hast slain
The flower of Europe for his chivalry;
And treacherously hast thou vanquished him,
For hand to hand he would have vanquished thee.
Now my soul's palace is become a prison;
Ah, would she break from hence, that this my body
Might in the ground be closèd up in rest,
For never henceforth shall I joy again.
Never, O never, shall I see more joy! [*He weeps.*]


RICHARD

I cannot weep, for all my body's moisture
Scarce serves to quench my furnace-burning heart;
Nor can my tongue unload my heart's great burden,
For selfsame wind that I should speak withal
Is kindling coals that fires all my breast
And burns me up with flames that tears would quench.
To weep is to make less the depth of grief:
Tears, then, for babes; blows and revenge for me.
Richard, I bear thy name. I'll venge thy death
Or die renownèd by attempting it.

William Shakespeare (1564-1616)

'the world stopped, lacking you'

From One Who Stays
Amy Lowell

# Remember

Remember me when I am gone away,
    Gone far away into the silent land;
    When you can no more hold me by the hand,
Nor I half turn to go yet turning stay.
Remember me when no more day by day
    You tell me of our future that you planned:
    Only remember me; you understand
It will be late to counsel then or pray.
Yet if you should forget me for a while
    And afterwards remember, do not grieve:
    For if the darkness and corruption leave
    A vestige of the thoughts that once I had,
Better by far you should forget and smile
Than that you should remember and be sad.

Christina Rossetti (1830–1894)

# The Old Familiar Faces

I have had playmates, I have had companions,
In my days of childhood, in my joyful school-days,
All, all are gone, the old familiar faces.

I have been laughing, I have been carousing,
Drinking late, sitting late, with my bosom cronies,
All, all are gone, the old familiar faces.

I loved a love once, fairest among women;
Closed are her doors on me, I must not see her –
All, all are gone, the old familiar faces.

I have a friend, a kinder friend has no man;
Like an ingrate, I left my friend abruptly;
Left him, to muse on the old familiar faces.

Ghost-like, I paced round the haunts of my childhood.
Earth seemed a desert I was bound to traverse,
Seeking to find the old familiar faces.

Friend of my bosom, thou more than a brother,
Why wert not thou born in my father's dwelling?
So might we talk of the old familiar faces –

How some they have died, and some they have left me,
And some are taken from me; all are departed;
All, all are gone, the old familiar faces.

Charles Lamb (1775-1834)

# Gone From My Sight

I am standing upon the seashore.
A ship, at my side, spreads her white
sails to the morning breeze and starts
for the blue ocean.

She is an object of beauty and strength.
I stand and watch her until, at length,
she hangs like a speck of white cloud
just where the sea and sky come
to mingle with each other.

Then, someone at my side says,
'There, she is gone.'

Gone where?

Gone from my sight. That is all.
She is just as large in mast, hull
and spar as she was when she left my side.
And, she is just as able to bear her
load of living freight to her destined port.
Her diminished size is in me – not in her.

And, just at the moment when someone
At my side, says, 'There, she is gone,'
there are other eyes watching her coming,
and other voices ready to take up the glad shout,
'Here she comes!'

And that is dying ...

Anon

# Kindness

Before you know what kindness really is
you must lose things,
feel the future dissolve in a moment
like salt in a weakened broth.
What you held in your hand,
what you counted and carefully saved,
all this must go so you know
how desolate the landscape can be
between the regions of kindness.
How you ride and ride
thinking the bus will never stop,
the passengers eating maize and chicken
will stare out the window forever.

Before you learn the tender gravity of kindness
you must travel where the Indian in a white poncho
lies dead by the side of the road.
You must see how this could be you,
how he too was someone
who journeyed through the night with plans
and the simple breath that kept him alive.

Before you know kindness as the deepest thing inside,
you must know sorrow as the other deepest thing.
You must wake up with sorrow.
You must speak to it till your voice
catches the thread of all sorrows
and you see the size of the cloth.
Then it is only kindness that makes sense anymore,
only kindness that ties your shoes
and sends you out into the day to gaze at bread,
only kindness that raises its head
from the crowd of the world to say
It is I you have been looking for,
and then goes with you everywhere
like a shadow or a friend.

**Naomi Shihab Nye (b.1952)**

# Deep in the Quiet Wood

Are you bowed down in heart?
Do you but hear the clashing discords and the din
  of life?
Then come away, come to the peaceful wood,
Here bathe your soul in silence. Listen! Now,
From out the palpitating solitude
Do you not catch, yet faint, elusive strains?
They are above, around, within you, everywhere.
Silently listen! Clear, and still more clear, they come.
They bubble up in rippling notes, and swell in
  singing tones.
Now let your soul run the whole gamut of the
  wondrous scale
Until, responsive to the tonic chord,
It touches the diapason of God's grand cathedral
  organ,
Filling earth for you with heavenly peace
And holy harmonies.

James Weldon Johnson (1871-1938)

# Praise the Rain

Praise the rain; the seagull dive
The curl of plant, the raven talk –
Praise the hurt, the house slack
The stand of trees, the dignity –
Praise the dark, the moon cradle
The sky fall, the bear sleep –
Praise the mist, the warrior name
The earth eclipse, the fired leap –
Praise the backwards, upward sky
The baby cry, the spirit food –
Praise canoe, the fish rush
The hole for frog, the upside-down –
Praise the day, the cloud cup
The mind flat, forget it all –

Praise crazy. Praise sad.
Praise the path on which we're led.
Praise the roads on earth and water.
Praise the eater and the eaten.
Praise beginnings; praise the end.
Praise the song and praise the singer.

Praise the rain; it brings more rain.
Praise the rain; it brings more rain.

Joy Harjo (b.1951)

'The same yet different, different yet the same'

Another and another and another
James Henry

# You must not shut the night inside you

From *Songs on the Death of Children*

You must not shut the night inside you,
But endlessly in light the dark immerse.
A tiny lamp has gone out in my tent –
I bless the flame that warms the universe.

Friedrich Rückert (1788–1866)

# No Coward Soul is Mine

No coward soul is mine
No trembler in the world's storm-troubled sphere:
I see Heaven's glories shine,
And Faith shines equal, arming me from Fear

O God within my breast,
Almighty ever-present Deity!
Life, that in me hast rest,
As I, Undying Life, have power in Thee!

Vain are the thousand creeds
That move men's hearts, unutterably vain;
Worthless as withered weeds,
Or idlest froth amid the boundless main,

To waken doubt in one
Holding so fast by Thy Infinity,
So surely anchored on
The steadfast rock of Immortality.

With wide-embracing love
Thy spirit animates eternal years
Pervades and broods above,
Changes, sustains, dissolves, creates and rears.

Though earth and moon were gone,
And suns and universes ceased to be,
And Thou wert left alone,
Every Existence would exist in Thee.

There is not room for Death,
Nor atom that his might could render void;
Thou – thou art Being and Breath,
And what thou art may never be destroyed.

Emily Brontë (1818-1848)

# Time, that renews the tissues of this frame

Time, that renews the tissues of this frame,
That built the child and hardened the soft bone,
Taught him to wail, to blink, to walk alone,
Stare, question, wonder, give the world a name,
Forget the watery darkness from whence he came,
Attends no less the boy to manhood grown,
Brings him new raiment, strips him of his own;
All skins are shed at length, remorse, even shame.
Such hope is mine, if this indeed be true,
I dread no more the first white in my hair,
Or even age itself, the easy shoe,
The cane, the wrinkled hands, the special chair:
Time, doing this to me, may alter too
My sorrow, into something I can bear.

Edna St. Vincent Millay (1892–1950)

# Time does not bring relief; you all have lied

Time does not bring relief; you all have lied
Who told me time would ease me of my pain!
I miss him in the weeping of the rain;
I want him at the shrinking of the tide;
The old snows melt from every mountain-side,
And last year's leaves are smoke in every lane;
But last year's bitter loving must remain
Heaped on my heart, and my old thoughts abide.
There are a hundred places where I fear
To go, – so with his memory they brim.
And entering with relief some quiet place
Where never fell his foot or shone his face
I say, 'There is no memory of him here!'
And so stand stricken, so remembering him.

Edna St. Vincent Millay (1892–1950)

# In mourning wise since daily I increase
Extract

In mourning wise since daily I increase,
Thus should I cloak the cause of all my grief:
So pensive mind with tongue to hold his peace
My reason sayeth there can be no relief;
Wherefore, give ear, I humbly you require,
The affects to know that thus doth make me moan.
The cause is great of all my doleful cheer
For those that were, and now be dead and gone.

What though to death desert be now their call
As by their faults it doth appear right plain.
Of force I must lament that such a fall
Should light on those so wealthily did reign,
Though some perchance will say, of cruel heart,
'A traitor's death why should we thus bemoan?'
But I alas, set this offence apart,
Must needs bewail the death of some be gone.
…
And thus, farewell, each one in hearty wise.
The axe is home, your heads be in the street.
The trickling tears doth fall so from my eyes,
I scarce may write, my paper is so wet.
But what can hope when death hath played his part
Though nature's course will thus lament and moan?
Leave sobs therefore, and every Christian heart
Pray for the souls of those be dead and gone.

Sir Thomas Wyatt (1503-1542)

# All is well
## From St Paul's Cathedral sermon, 1910

Death is nothing at all.
It does not count.
I have only slipped away into the next room.
Everything remains exactly as it was.
I am I, and you are you, and the old life that we lived
  so fondly together is untouched, unchanged.
Whatever we were to each other, that we are still.
Call me by the old familiar name.
Speak of me in the easy way which you always used.
Put no difference into your tone.
Wear no forced air of solemnity or sorrow.
Laugh as we always laughed at the little jokes that we
  enjoyed together.
Play, smile, think of me, pray for me.
Let my name be ever the household word that it
  always was.
Let it be spoken without an effort, without the ghost
  of a shadow upon it.
Life means all that it ever meant.
It is the same as it ever was.
There is absolute and unbroken continuity.
Why should I be out of mind because I am out of sight?
I am but waiting for you, for an interval, somewhere
  very near, just round the corner.
All is well.

Henry Scott Holland (1847–1918)

# Twilight
(Nahant)

There was an evening when the sky was clear,
    Ineffably translucent in its blue;
    The tide was falling, and the sea withdrew
In hushed and happy music from the sheer
Shadowy granite of the cliffs; and fear
    Of what life may be, and what death can do,
    Fell from us like steel armor, and we knew
The beauty of the Law that holds us here.
It was as though we saw the Secret Will,
    It was as though we floated and were free;
      In the south-west a planet shone serenely,
      And the high moon, most reticent and queenly,
Seeing the earth had darkened and grown still,
    Misted with light the meadows of the sea.

Sara Teasdale (1884–1933)

'Love,
faithful
love,
recalled
thee to
my mind'

**Surprised by Joy**
William Wordsworth

# Into the Hour

I have come into the hour of a white healing.
Grief's surgery is over and I wear
The scar of my remorse and of my feeling.

I have come into a sudden sunlit hour
When ghosts are scared to corners. I have come
Into the time when grief begins to flower

Into a new love. It had filled my room
Long before I recognised it. Now
I speak its name. Grief finds its good way home.

The apple-blossom's handsome on the bough
and Paradise spreads round. I touch its grass.
I want to celebrate but don't know how.

I need not speak though everyone I pass
Stares at me kindly. I would put my hand
Into their hands. Now I have lost my loss

In some way I may later understand.
I hear the singing of the Summer grass
And love, I find, has no considered end,

Nor is it subject to the wilderness
Which follows death. I am not traitor to
A person or a memory. I trace

Behind that love another which is running
Around, ahead. I need not ask its meaning.

Elizabeth Jennings (1926–2001)

# Another and another and another

Another and another and another
And still another sunset and sunrise,
The same yet different, different yet the same,
Seen by me now in my declining years
As in my early childhood, youth and manhood;
And by my parents and my parents' parents,
And by the parents of my parents' parents,
And by their parents counted back for ever,
Seen, all their lives long, even as now by me;
And by my children and my children's children
And by the children of my children's children
And by their children counted on for ever
Still to be seen as even now seen by me;
Clear and bright sometimes, sometimes dark and
  clouded
But still the same sunsetting and sunrise;
The same for ever to the never ending
Line of observers, to the same observer
Through all the changes of his life the same:
Sunsetting and sunrising and sunsetting,
And then again sunrising and sunsetting,
Sunrising and sunsetting evermore.

James Henry (1798–1876)

# 'The sun rises in spite of everything'

**Everything Is Going to Be All Right**
Derek Mahon

# Index (Author Names)

# Index (First Lines)

# Sources

**Denise Levertov:**
'Talking to Grief' by Denise Levertov, from POEMS
  1972-1982,copyright ©1978 by Denise Levertov.
  Reprinted by permission of New Directions Publishing
  Corp. Denise Levertov New Selected Poems (Bloodaxe
  Books, 2003). Reproduced with permission of Bloodaxe
  Books www.bloodaxebooks.com @bloodaxebooks
  (twitter/facebook) #bloodaxebooks

**Derek Mahon:**
By kind permission of Estate of Derek Mahon and The
  Gallery Press, Loughcrew, Oldcastle, County Meath,
  Ireland from The Poems:1961-2020 (2021).

**Elizabeth Jennings:**
'I Count the Moments of my Mercies Up' and 'Into the
  Hour' from The Collected Poems by Elizabeth Jennings
  (Carcanet Press); reproduced by permission of David
  Higham Associates.

**Emily Dickinson:**
THE POEMS OF EMILY DICKINSON: READING
  EDITION, edited by Ralph W. Franklin, Cambridge,
  Mass.: The Belknap Press of Harvard University Press,
  Copyright © 1998, 1999 by the President and Fellows
  of Harvard College. Copyright © 1951, 1955 by the
  President and Fellows of Harvard College. Copyright
  © renewed 1979, 1983 by the President and Fellows
  of Harvard College. Copyright © 1914, 1918, 1919,
  1924, 1929, 1930, 1932, 1935, 1937, 1942 by Martha
  Dickinson Bianchi. Copyright © 1952, 1957, 1958, 1963,

## Acknowledgements

A very big thank you to the great team at Batsford, particularly to my editors Magda Simões-Brown and Nicola Newman. Thank you, as ever, to The Reader charity for not only reigniting my own love of literature but also showing me, through the practice of shared reading and reading aloud, how to help people overcome the barriers that sometimes stand in the way of us enjoying and experiencing poetry. Thank you to my family and friends who continue to support and encourage my literary adventures.

## About the Editor

Liz Ison studied English Literature at the University of Cambridge. Since 2015, Liz has been leading shared reading groups in person and online as well as workshops encouraging people to enjoy and rediscover poetry. Her poetry anthologies include *A Poem to Read Aloud Every Day of the Year* and *Poems for Tortured Souls*. Liz lives in London.

First published in the United Kingdom
in 2025 by
Batsford
43 Great Ormond Street
London
WC1N 3HZ

An imprint of B. T. Batsford Holdings Limited

ISBN 978 1 84994 962 0

A CIP catalogue record for this book is available from the
British Library.

10 9 8 7 6 5 4 3 2 1

Printed by Toppan Leefung Printing International Ltd, China
Reproduction by Rival Colour Ltd, UK

This book can be ordered direct from the publisher at
www.batsfordbooks.com, or try your local bookshop

MIX
Paper | Supporting
responsible forestry
FSC
www.fsc.org
FSC® C104723